LISTEN
to the SUNRISE

Hymns and Prayers

Kenneth I. Morse

faithQuest
Elgin, IL

Listen to the Sunrise
Hymns and Prayers by Kenneth I. Morse

Acknowledgements: Burning Bush, Something Like a
Tree, When I Consider, Direction, A Star Went Before, The
Garden, April, so Autumn Comes, October, Drum,
Together, Today, Window, Listen, Friend, We Must Join
Hands, Answer, Images of Hope, Listen to the Sunrise,
An Advent Song, The Face of Love, Season of Faith, A
Rose in Winter, Bethlehem, When Love Was Born, The
Gift of Grace are reprinted from *Messenger* with
permission.

Cover Art by Janie Russell
Cover Design by Jeane Healy

Manufactured in the United States of America

for
Marjorie

CONTENTS

Introduction

Several years ago I heard an artist describe what became for me a new understanding of effective communication. The artist said, "I strive to create a work of integrity and beauty—a song, a clay pot, a poem, a painting, a building, a story, a design—but that work has significance only if it becomes a gift I can share with one person or many. My creation may be interpreted differently by those who accept it. They may or may not feel the emotions that prompted me. They may discover meanings in my work that never occurred to me. Communication happens when you are willing to entrust something that represents a part of yourself into the welcoming hands of another."

It is in this context, of sharing a personal gift, that I commend this book to readers. I am aware that many of the poems and a few of the hymns betray their journalistic origins in church publications. They are bound to reflect the winds of doctrine and currents of controversy of the last fifty years. The earliest poem is a meditation for Christmas Eve, 1940, when our country was preparing to conscript its young men to serve in a war that came a year later. The most recent poem is a text for an Advent hymn for December, 1990, another time of darkness brought on by the threat of war.

I make no apology for serious concerns that surface in these lines, for they reflect my most deeply held convictions about faith and life. But I hope the reader will find here also something to enjoy for its own sake: some song with a music all its own; some image to launch a reverie; some blending of words with the silences between them; some wisps of memory to release a shower of recollections; or some rhyme to ring like the echo of a distant bell. This is the best gift poetry can offer, a way to release the words and the music in your own heart.

The eternal God, who gave us the most precious gift in the person of a Son, communicated a love beyond all knowing. That glory grows—and glows—all around us. So listen to the sunrise.

Kenneth I. Morse
February, 1991

I. BIRDS, TREES, STARS AND OTHER MIRACLES

 *BURNING BUSH*

A hundred times I walked that way,
past weathered barns, by rotting railroad ties
where flowers grew as wild as weeds.
A hundred times I stopped to watch
creek waters curl and wash a willow tree,
then pause to dance in the warmth of the sun.
A hundred times I heard the earth sigh,
and I waited for a whisper in the wind.

Then one day, a day no different than the others,
here in the midst of my accustomed places,
I saw the miracle, the light within a light.
A tree flamed with a thousand fires,
defying death and brightly reaffirming
its right to be consumed and live again.
I heard a voice, like tempered thunder,
explain that God needs no explaining.
God is who God is.
Everything else is commentary.
God is. Is that not miracle enough?

And I am who I am, awed by this wonder.
I am who I am, standing naked in this light.
The places I have walked
a hundred times, unseeing,
are all God's holy ground.   (1982)

REPLY

Touch the root
where it investigates the soil.
Look long at the leaf
where it reaches for the way of the wind.
Be kind to the branch
where it bends like an artery of life.
Trace the pattern
of earthy shapes and colors
silhouetted against the sky.
And ask your questions
of whence and whither and why.
This tree is its own reply.   (1984)

AN AGING OAK

An aging oak—bent, battered, bruised by storms—
now twisted into wild and weird contortions,
leans hard against the canyon's steep incline,
unwilling to revoke its right to thrust
more browning branches, gestured in defiance,
into the open country of young pines.

Like a mighty torso, wrought in agony,
its tormented trunk draws vigor from the land.
Time after time discarded branches crash
and crumble, proving death is always near.
But yet there comes the greening of an arm held high
and strength enough to point a finger to the sky.
                                               (1989)

Something like a tree
    is shadowed on the sky.
Is this the time for hope to die?
No, the tree blossoms—
    and you hear a cry:
Alleluia!   (1971)

REDWOODS

They have lived so long,
in dignity conferred by centuries,
they scarcely notice, pressing to the sky,
the lower ranks of younger trees
who starve for sunlight in their shade.

They have seen so much:
changes in shoreline, all that wild winds do;
the worst of weather, best of time;
the birth and end of nations, all things passing;
so much of horror, hid or undisguised;
so much of beauty, viewed in mild surprise;
so much that shakes and shames, then fades away.

They have grown so well,
towering as if to be forever
the imperturbable masters of the land they claim,
superior in vision, resting firm on mountainsides,
Yet comes one day, though ages yet away, a day
for each in crashing thunder to end its history.
The redwoods write their own obituaries, ring by ring;
they show time pushing toward eternity.
                                       (1989)

THE WAY OF WINGS

Try, if you can, to follow the path of one bird;
try without dropping your eyes or falling behind.
Trace, if you can, each gentle spiral, each swelling arc,
each lovely lifting from flower to telephone wire.
Who could program a pattern so daringly woven
of sweeping curves, sharp bends, sudden and daring
    dives?
You will envy this creature not its flash of color
so much as its being at home in the arms of the wind.
And you will marvel at unpredictable journeys
across trackless waters and over the tops of trees.
Freedom and song belong to this way of wings,
this love affair with the earth and the sky.

                            (1981)

MORNING SONG

Scarcely had velvet clouds appeared
    Above the east, before the sun;
Scarcely had shades of darkness cleared
    To say the new day had begun;
When bursting from the hills around
    A hundred trees broke into song;
A thousand voices joined to sound
    A hymn of praise serene and strong.

If songbirds joining in the praise
    Of God's own creatures can invite
Nature's whole symphony to raise
    A choral greeting to the light,
Let us who know God's mercies, then,
    Be early in our morning prayer,
And let us lift now and again
    Our songs of faith into the air.   (1944)

WHEN I CONSIDER

They center in but circle yet—
a sea of stars, less distant, friendlier.
Only in awe can I respect their nearness.
For when my mind considers measuring the heavens,
miles vanish into years and yield to ages.
Would any dare so recklessly to spend
a lifetime estimating this immensity
only to find it swallowed up in vaster spaces?
Or yet to learn it is no more
than one brief breath exhaled
light years ago and long forgotten?

But for my heart's horizon I accept no boundaries.
A tear contains a thousand galaxies.
And I—the least, lone, last invited guest—
May walk in wonder up and down the Milky Way.

(1971)

DIRECTION

Across the dome of sky
this day spins
picking up pieces of pain
silencing agonies
and twisting iridescent happenings
into a fabric that fades from noon to night.

O wind that wraps the world,
how many loves move you
to circumscribe and turn this sphere
earthbound, yet heavenward? (1970)

A STAR WENT BEFORE THEM

Only one star,
one light, one way . . .
when out of all God's universes
spanning both space and time
there must be myriad beams
leaping from sun to sun,
on to eternal day?

I cannot know what dreams
attract uncounted hearts in other worlds,
or how diverse the visions that illuminate
another's mind.

I only know my desperate need to find
one star ahead,
lighting my path
one step along one way.   (1964)

LIKE STAR, LIKE TREE

Like moon, like star,
like tree you are;
 given one place,
 that place you grace.
  Like star, like tree,
  so must you be
   firm like the earth
   that gave you birth.

Like earth, like sky,
like dusk you lie
 peaceful in rest
 when dark is best.
  Like wind, like rain
  you hide your pain
   away from sight
   like leaves at night.

Like wave, like wood—
all God makes good—
 you bend to give,
 you stretch to live.
  Like soil, like sand
  you understand
   why you should be
   like star, like tree.   (1979)

 *LEVELED WORLD*

A dun gray sky,
spread like rough jelly on a low ceiling,
horizontals my view.

On a day so soft, the air the earth breathes
    seems almost to cease.
In a world so leveled my eyes move in circumferences,
    never up or down.
Distant sounds disappear and quiet is stifling.
A bird's shrill shriek or the wash of an ominous wave
    would be welcome evidence of life.

For what purpose is the sky flattened,
    the shore evened, the waters stilled?
Is the earth being hushed to hear a cry?

When will the vertical vision of shattering sunlight
    split the heavens, trouble the waves,
    bring me a startling wonder, a revelation?
When will the open lake be written upon
    with a message, a summons, a call?

When the sky shouts, will I waken
    from the somnolence of this dark serenity
    to live again, to leap up, to sing,
    to crack the solid silence with a cry?

Peace, yes, but not this crust of death.
Let me pierce it with an alleluia
    even if the lightning
    and the thunder
    come again.   (1979)

THE GARDEN

The Lord God planted a garden.
The Lord God gave us a land
Where trees in loveliest grandeur grew
By streams of water as fresh as dew,
And the air we breathed was ever new.
We could open our eyes
In a paradise
For the Lord had planted a garden.

But we have corrupted that garden,
　　And we have wasted that land.
　　Our poisons peril each leaf and blade.
　　Our earth is scarred, and its beauties fade.
　　Our air is heavy with a death we made,
　　And a darkening pall
Hangs over all
Like a shadow across God's garden.

O brothers, we see our own judgment.
O sisters, we stumble toward death.
The garden we lost we may regain.
We can salvage the life we would sustain,
But love must grace the earth again,
And humanity's need
Must supplant our greed.
O God, send your cleansing rain!　　　(1969)

 **WHILE IT RAINS**

red cliffs frame for memory
a moist and misty day:

hovering horizons
lower like dropping-down clouds
filled with frosty-fog rain

our compact car cuts
softly through wetness
witnessed and blessed
by watery maples and birches
benching all beaches

and thousands of trees
say hello
and throw kisses
that keep our windshield
wetter than tears

we are happy when branches
brush us and wave us on
by harbors and harbingers
into a harvest
only the heart knows

wet red rocks
circle the pools
that contentment contains
and we wait
wet but glad
glad but wet
while it rains

CLERMONT: LA PLUIE

The sky is so troubled it weeps.
Abundant tears overflow,
washing our windows while we wait
for the winds to whip by
and the sun to smile—tomorrow.

Gardens drink heavily of the rain.
Intoxicated, they flourish and bloom
while the grass deepens
its soft green carpet,
moist and clean.

Reach up to the rain.
Let it nourish your heart like a spring
rising from the good earth
for all children of God to drink
and be satisfied.   (1985)

COLORS ON THE RAIN

With love of friends to strengthen and sustain,
My heart will have its triumph over pain.
I can be sure my waiting's not in vain
When scattered pieces fall in place again.
    God's bow still spreads its colors on the rain.

 ## APRIL

If any month be heaven,
it must be April, given
to a winter-hardened race
in charity and grace
lest we too soon forget
God is our maker yet.

With feeling April yields
a tearful warmth to fields,
her yellowing and greening
a miracle of meaning;
and April's earth, forgiven,
resembles April's heaven. (1969)

SO AUTUMN COMES

Mature and bending,
broken with the burden of bearing,
so autumn comes with fragile frost,
the servant season. (1968)

OCTOBER

October holds the future in its hands.
Are wispy seeds, falling and faltering,
too vulnerable to storms?
Ah, there the latent beauty lies,
trustingly waiting to be blown
and sown.

Comes October's coverlet of color,
rich with sunlight, soft in rain;
time to set the future free
for flight and rest—and then to be
born again.   (1976)

APOLOGY

Excuse me, earth.
Forgive me for scarring your face
and forgetting your part
in giving me birth
and a place
to grow in the sun.

 **WORDS**

Give me an alphabet
of letters straight and stern,
leaning into laughter.

Typographers should form them
fanciful but firm;
calligraphers should find them
meek but also mighty.

Give me words to work a wonder
even when they walk precisely.
Writers should fashion them
faithful to fact
but waiting with wings.   (1982)

WHISPER AND WORD

Job 26:14

Great are the monuments that mountains raise
Through cloud and mist to hymn the Lord God's praise,
And greater still the lonely majesty
Of mirrored stars across an endless sea—
 Lo, these are but the outskirts of his ways;
 How small a whisper do we hear of him!

Vast are the reaches of unmeasured space
Where suns and satellites their courses trace,
Where newly visioned worlds of wonder share
The glories that familiar heavens declare—
 Lo, these are but the outskirts of his ways;
 How small a whisper do we hear of him!

How small a whisper—yet how firm the voice
That speaking through creation says, "Rejoice!"
The thunder of God's power rolls again
In judgment on our barren regimen.
But hear the sound that breaks across the sky
In Bethlehem to mark a baby's cry;
And heed the words that rise from Calvary,
Laden with love for all humanity—
No whispers these, for we at last have heard
God speak in Christ the everlasting Word.

       (1960)

 *THE GIFT OF A DAY*

I can feel the orange glow of the sun
that drops by trellis and lattice
in lacy patterns across my bed.
I can rise now and throw off the clothing of night.
Each particle of sunlight is an offering
from the golden store of resurrection,
to be hailed with silent alleluias
in the early hours of each new day.
Almost all my fears dissolve in the radiance
that sweeps around me; almost all anxieties
leave with the shadows when they disappear.
Yet some uncertainties remain, to hold in tension
night with day and calm with storm,
the edge of guilt that rims tranquility.

But what a prospect lies in any day:
miracles of growth, the exhilaration of beauty,
a tempest at midday and serenity at sunset.
The air teems with possibilities;
the framing of our visions still expands;
and we are blessed with a gift we can never deserve
in the gift of a day that renews itself
in the gift of love.   (1985)

A SONG IN THE NIGHT

(Isa. 30:29)

The air is stretched thin like a transparent ribbon.
What I hear is what I shall never see:
the texture of a music invisibly moving
beyond the ranges of anticipation.
What I hear is a song, a salutation,
an utterance of joy, a celebration.

From the flute a shower of liquid notes
tumbles and spills like a flowing fountain.
From the heart, happy and generous, rises a flood,
the lovely liftings of sound, upraising in praise,
more festive than anthems and alleluias.
A song in the night, a feast, a setting forth
to the holiest of sacred mountains.
A cry of joy: our God is our salvation.
O pilgrims, let me join your chorus.
Your flute is more certain than my trumpet.
I follow where its music leads.   (1979)

II. Love Is the Drummer

 ## DRUM

If I could
there are times I would
still the drum,
soften its beat,
silence its sound,
slow it down.

But life says the pulse must pound,
the rhythm may falter but must not cease,
and even in rest there is no release.
Life says the beat must lean
into tomorrow, strong and clean;
and love says life is right;
and God says love is the drummer
who never sleeps.   (1970)

TOGETHER

We walked together, you and I,
wherever we wanted to walk
without ever whispering a word.

   Yet your heart I heard,
   and I caught you measuring my mind.

You and I—
we never will discover how
we understand in silence,
but we know why.   (1969)

TODAY

Let yesterday go.
Say yes to today.

Today is God's finger
creating the world anew
and touching you.

Today is God's offer of life,
the miracle and mystery
of being uniquely you,
in this place
and at this time,
today.

Today
is the room
where you and I stand
with all our brothers and sisters,
hopefully hand in hand
in the wide-open world
of today.

Today is the door
God opens into eternity.
Thank you, God,
for today.   (1969)

 **WINDOWS**

Open
whatever windows wait
to let life in.

There is a seed in the wind
far too infinitesimal
ever to be evident.

Your bandages may guard against infection.
You may turn inner space into a vacuum.
You may secure your emptiness
    by barring every door,
    sealing every window,
    barricading exits and entrances
    to your personal fortress,
    gaining a guarantee
    of protection and perfection,
    serenity and order,
    the order of death.

Or you can be vulnerable
to the infectious injuries
of love.

Open whatever windows wait
to let life in.   (1969)

LOOKING AT YOU

Looking at you
I must first forget
conventional categories
and the convenient compartments
where I might file you
and index you by page and number.
I must forget all such data
and look at you simply,
look at you openly,
look at you for the first time
as if God had newly created you,
as indeed God did, uniquely.

Looking at you
I find you delightfully unpredictable,
defying any description.
    You void my analysis,
    you confound my prejudices,
    you upset my defenses,
    you resist my manipulations,
    for you are yourself, no other . . .
That is why I intend to keep on
looking at you.

 ## *LISTEN, FRIEND*

It is more than a sound;
it is someone's song that you hear.
So listen, friend.

Listen to a bee's humming . . . and
    to the wrenching ring of tires that
    burn down a hot highway.

Listen to a bird's fluting . . . and
    to the ambulance siren wailing its way
    up some street of sorrows.

Listen to a kitten's purring . . . and
    to the grinding gears of a mad machine
    churning out progress.

Listen to a lover's lullaby . . . and
    to the whip of hurricane winds that
    waste both land and water.

Listen to a mother's praying . . . and
    to the cries of motherless children who
    hunger for a heart to hold them.

Always it is someone's song that you hear.
So listen, friend.   (1969)

WE MUST JOIN HANDS

I cannot stretch my arms enough
to measure all God gives to me.
I need your arms—and hers and his—
to compass what God offers me
out of great generosity.
We must join hands
to worship thankfully.   (1969)

A WEDDING SONG

(for Jan and David)

You shall have a song
when morning rims the mountains
and sun-fresh stillness melts the night away.
So let your singing hearts
light up the sky with laughter
while music marks the blooming of your day.

You shall have a song
when every touch is tender
and voices speak the language of your love.
So let your eager eyes
behold the birth of beauty
and watch with wonder where the planets move.

   Speak soft, speak low
   in whispers measured to the night.
   Sing out—and shout
   the glories of your hearts' delight.

For you shall have a song,
a symphony of gladness,
to help you find the paths where you belong.
So may you trust God's grace
to guide your life together
in sun and shadow—you shall have a song.

(1988)

ANNA ROSE, AT THREE MONTHS

That day when you were christened Anna Rose,
strong arms hoisted your tiny body high
so you could see at once the open skies
matching the depth and color of your eyes.
But God returned you to your parents' arms
for nurturing and nesting, safe from harms.
Cradled in love, you sleep and stretch and cry,
hallowing your home with smile or sigh.

Already, Anna, you can clearly see
faces of friends known in community.
From arm to arm you're often passed,
by each one held in love, by each one blessed.
Early you learn the gift of being treasured;
you are accepted with a joy unmeasured.
God blesses your extended family
and welcomes you to their community.

So richly loved, you can but grow in grace
while miracles surround your time and place.
The promise of a life abundant flows
around you and within you, Anna Rose.

(1989)

 **MOTHERS**

Warm, whirring wings appear to hover
over the nest they almost cover,
and gaping throats reach up in trust
that food will come, as come it must.
For such a hunger as you see
a mother is sufficiency.

Winds rip and roar around each nest,
fragile as straw but woven fast.
Rain fills the air and bends the tree—
a mother is security.

Let bird-songs rise and wings go free.
For love to guide humanity
a mother is necessity.   (1988)

LINES FOR A WEDDING ANNIVERSARY

We are tender and sometimes trailing vines,
born of distinct and diverted branches,
who remember the uniqueness of their roots.
We have been brushed and blown by sharp winds,
yet firmly joined in the peace of God's rain,
so that our leaves can intertwine,
our prospects interweave, our hearts combine.

Around one giant tree we grow together,
interleaved and interwrought by fingers
that fashioned us into what we have become.
We can be as strong as that tree of faith
that supports, sustains, and molds us;
as vulnerable as the most fragile flower
blooming alone in a corner of God's creation;
as happy indeed as all those who sleep
under the Lord's benediction.   (1987)

 **CERTAINTIES**

They took the signpost down
when the bulldozer stopped at the corner.
I saw it and I knew I must remap
territories in my mind.

I fear some memories are obsolete,
recalling landscapes brushed by winds
too fierce to let a landmark stand.

O where are certainties?
Today's rose loses half its loveliness
to rain—and will not bloom again.
Tomorrow all my gardens will have gone
to grace some neighbor's wilderness.

So what is firm?
Whose fence is fixed?
I read new versions, find no final text.
Are there no boundaries closer than galaxies
stretching in stars?

Come. Let me take your hand.

INTO A PATTERN

Into a pattern of praise and prayer
Our hearts can gather the threads of each day,
Lifting the strands of joy and care,
Weaving a life as we work and play.

God of each color, each bright design,
God of the loom on which they spread,
God of the eyes that search each line,
God of the hand that shuttles the thread,

Bless now our striving, our toil, our rest;
Accept the labors of all our days.
Guide every thread that is drawn and pressed
Into a pattern to sing your praise.   (1950)

MOMENTS ARE MEASURED

An hour, a minute, a year, a day—
number them well; they never stay
longer than counting can hold them still.
They cannot return; they never will.

A minute, an hour, a day, a year—
From past to present, from there to here
life's moments are measured, then cease to be.
They offer us bits of eternity.

So live them well, for each is a gift
For love to use when time is swift;
And each is a song, if you think it so,
For love to sing when time is slow.

BIRTHDAY ARITHMETIC

How many suns and how many moons?
How many plates and how many spoons?
How many "too lates," how many "too soons"?

How many days and how many years?
How many laughs and how many tears?
How much by faith and how much by fears?

How many minutes and how many hours?
How many stars and how many flowers?
How much is "mine" and how much is "ours"?

How many winters and how many springs?
How many kisses and how many stings?
Count all of it joy if still your heart sings.

(1982)

REMEMBERING LOULOU

Like a flower
that will not yield to fading
but glows with a radiance all its own
even after its petals start to fall,
she blossomed with perennial kindness
in all our gardens; and our hearts
were warmed with her welcomes,
from "Bon jour" to "Bonne nuit."   (1988)

LEARN FROM LOVE

Learn from love how to sing;
Learn from faith how to fly;
Learn from God how to live;
Learn from life how to die.

ANSWERS

I prayed for answers,
    but only the questions came clear.
I asked for release,
    but instead my journey was lengthened.
I yearned for achievement,
    but I was given the grace of disappointment.
I demanded some assurance
    but certainty was lacking.

What God offered me was love
    and a hand in mine for the taking
    and great joy
    and deep pain
    and a lonely walk in the way of a cross.
What God offered was life.
It was more then I prayed for.   (1969)

A BREAK IN TIME

A break in time
for eternity to shine through.
A crack in the wall
for flowers to root and grow.
A glance to one side
for an admission of guilt.
A pause in the play
for words not in the script.
A step out of line
for actions not planned in the march.
A lapse in the day
for items overlooked in the agenda.

A break in time
for God to speak,
for a word from a cross,
for the world to be shaken
by love's interruption.

IMAGES OF HOPE

HOPE
a joy
a rock
a song
a child
a hand upon a door
a firm foundation
a sun, a star, a sky
a day at dawn, an exaltation

HOPE
an arm
a rope, a ladder
a target and an arrow
a circle of sisters and brothers

HOPE
an anchor
a gift of grace
a miracle, a marvel
a voice, a vision, an ecstacy
a prayer, a path, a promise
an act of God, an intervention
a taste of love, a touch of heaven
a celebration

HOPE   (1970)

III. Listen to the Sunrise

1. The Ninth Hour

It is a time to be afraid.

See how the sky drops its face,
how clouds knit their brows.
The hills hide any sign of kindness
and the clustering darkness frowns
even though it is only midafternoon.

O black, silent sky,
what omens do you carry?
When will the thunder break
to release the tension
of apprehension and anxiety?

And where has the sun gone?
Is the hero of the sky hiding somewhere,
afraid to stride again boldly
across the burning heavens
from his rising to his setting?
It is a time to be afraid.

Heaven lowers its burden on the earth
while menacing shadows search out
all the city's streets,
announcing the presence of fear.

2. Earth Tremors

It is a time to be anxious.

Even the earth trembles.
Its surface shivers and shakes.
The waters shimmer.
The forest slips,
rocks split apart,
streets divide,
crevices appear in a country road,
buildings totter,
curtains tear,
children whimper,
and mothers cry in terror.
Surely God is also shaken.
Has God now forsaken us?
The world seems unbalanced.
There is a darkness at noon
and a strange brightness at midnight.
Someone nearby whispers,
"What if God is dying, or already dead?"
The thought unnerves me
even more than the fear of the dark
or the unsettling shaking of the earth.

I listen to a new lament
like the sighing and the singing
of the daughters of Jerusalem
who even now, this dark day,
weep for themselves
and for their children.

3. Lament of a Contemporary

You know how it is now . . .

The judge on the bench has been indicted.
The makers of laws bend them to their own advantage.
The guardians of the peace collaborate
    with those who threaten.
There is murder in broad daylight
    and no witnesses will testify.
A woman is attacked but no one heeds her cry.
The innocent pay while the transgressor goes free.
The young are restless, impatient with a world
    they did not choose.
Public words speak of peace,
    but secret papers rattle with schemes of violence.
The casualties of warmaking are no longer only
    on the field of battle.
The bloodletting has come home to us,
    and we are neighbors to our victims.
The enemy looks at us from a mirror,
    but we continue to bomb the fields of our friends.
Nor has the earth escaped the pollution of our spirit.
We have alienated a generation of the living.
    And we prescribe a barren world
    for generations yet unborn.

You know how it is now . . .

Once we followed leaders
    but now we must choose among images.
Once we could speak face to face
    but now we respond to lines on a screen.
Once we gathered to hear the songs of our tradition,
    but now we are lonely listeners,
        missing each other's voices in the dark.

Once we knew the warm ties of family,
    but now we are bitter and hungry for love.
Once we marveled at the miracle of creation,
    but now we have lost the picture of a God who lives
    and moves in a world of wonder.

There were darknesses before,
but now the sun is so overcast
it is difficult any longer to see
the silhouette of three black crosses
on a hill—and the hill is so far away.

4. There Is No Out

So, I run here and away
among strangers and friends,
hoping they will reassure me.
I look for someone to say,
   "Do not fear, do not fly,
    the sun also rises, darkness must go,
    after one day, a second day, a third day
    God will return, and love will reign . . ."
But so many say, "No,
   this midnight is forever.
   The only light is at the end of the establishment.
   The only order is anarchy.
   The only meaning is the reality of misery."
They quench their fears with anger.
They answer anxiety with resentment.
They have only a hell and no hope of heaven,
and they wearily advocate ingenious ways
of dropping out,
copping out,
opting out.
But there is no out.

5. *If God Is Dead*

If God is dead,
overcome by the evil
God might have prevented but did not—

If God is dead,
rejected by the persons God loved,
tried and sentenced in the name of religion,
crucified as a threat to security,
tormented as a troublemaker—

If God is dead—
then the deepening darkness is explainable
and the coldness of the silent earth
is appropriate.

If God is dead,
let us at least bury Jesus in a lovely garden
and seal his tomb for the duration;
for it will be a long hard season,
and the Sabbath will come and go without any sound,
if God is dead.

If.

6. Interruptions in the Silence

No night is ever total.
Somewhere a candle flames,
flickers, sputters, steadies,
beaming ever-widening waves of timid light
into surprising circumferences.

Or here and there
a restless sleeper pulls back
curtains draping blackness
and looks tentatively into the ebony
dome of night, inquiring about stars.

The distant suns, away by years, are there.
Like the pricking of pin points,
one by one they communicate light
while drawing blood.
So intimations of life break
into the most solemn wake
for the dead.

If you listen, you know.
Thin reedy sounds, like distant flutes,
interrupt the heaviest silence.

And who can number the seeds
that sleep beneath the snow?

7. Listen to the Sunrise

Listen to the sunrise.
Surely you must hear clouds moving
when canyons split and open to the sun.

Listen to the sunrise.
Be sensitive to stones
shaken by the daybreak.
One rumble of the dawn
can root a rock and start it rolling,
picking up pieces of thunder on the way.

Listen to the sunrise.
Listen to the sharp, bright morning.
Listen to the first and glorious day.
Listen to the sound of a heartbeat
    announcing in the womb of winter
    that out of darkness,
    out of dying,
    out of midnight,
    out of sorrow and travail
God is bringing light to life,
God is bringing life to light.
Listen to the sunrise.
Listen to the first and glorious day.

8. Flower in the Rock

From out that hostile stone
I least expected life to come.
But there, impossibly, blooms one fragile flower.

Against all arguments a flower flames
where reasonably it should not be,
barricading tombs with beauty.
Must God waste minor miracles
on pessimists and doubters just like me?

I could trample and crush that flower,
dismember it, chill it with unconcern,
yet there it is,
blooming as trustingly
as if all heaven sustained it
and verified its joy.
Yes, there one flower blooms,
earth-rooted, opening to the sky—
and where am I?

9. Bird Flight

Watching birds in flight
is listening to a language
no one yet has learned to read.

They carve wild patterns from each sky
with every swerve, whip, glide, or dive.
Their winged ways curve gently
like the flow of poetry
and they speak of faith
such as an earth-bound creature seldom knows.
They trust in currents felt
but never seen,
invisibly available to wings.

I tremble at small heights.
So heavy is my heart
that gravity inclines me toward the grave.

But birds are risen, free.
Released in space they track new orbits,
circumscribe expanding arcs,
and weave their wonder into skies.
Watching birds in flight, even I can trace
the moving of God's grace.

10. Every Time a Child

Every time a child is born,
   death yields a fraction of its power.
Every time a baby cries,
   despair has less to say to me.
Every time a mother speaks her lullaby,
   faith looks up from faltering.
Every step a child takes for the first time
   opens a highway through the heart's jungle.
Every word a child speaks for the first time
   starts a shout to waken us from slumber.
Every hand a child waves in innocent delight
   offers an invitation to tomorrow.
Every time a child smiles back at God,
   I take courage.
   Death may be responsible for endings.
   It has no victory.

11. Walking in the Resurrection

His friends were reluctant conscripts for the
ministry of death, but instead he said Yes to life
so firmly he went to prison and so gently that
the judge was moved. He still endures mild
crucifixions, but he spreads eternity wherever
he walks. . . .

She never saw them—those impossible pupils—after
they matured enough to discover they loved her,
but the values she lived became a part of their
heritage. Unmarried, alone, in weakening health,
she is half-forgotten by the generations
she nursed into adulthood. . . .

Shy, timid, sometimes fearful, this young mother is
the one who cared enough to write a public letter,
to speak at town meeting, to answer
threatening phone calls, to risk her leisure, to
disturb someone's evil peace. God helping her,
she could do no other. . . .

The outcasts call him their friend, and he hardly
knows why he lets them find him, for they have
shaded his reputation. But he remembers the day
a Christ-figure touched him and turned him
around. There is a joy in his limp that comes
from walking in the resurrection.

12. God's Moment Has Come

It is time to awaken.
There is a fire in the sky.
High over eastern horizons
rises the amber flame
that will flood the world with light.

Awake and see the marvel of morning.
Reach up and touch the transformation.
There is a new radiance, an electrifying energy.
You can hear the sunrise break into alleluias.

God's moment has come.
This is the first day of the week,
the first day of countless new lives,
the first day of a new order and a new age.
The time of God's visitation
is the time of our liberation.

Listen to the sunrise.
Listen to the sharp, bright morning.
Listen to the first and glorious day.
God is bringing light to life.
God is bringing life to light.
Listen to the sunrise, and rejoice!

IV. Season of Joy

AN ADVENT SONG

Waits the world in darkness, full of fear.
Waits the world in wonder: is God near?
Waits the world for glory to appear,
    Waiting for Immanuel.

Comes a Song to open heaven's skies.
Comes a Child to hear our mortal cries.
Comes a Star to show us where He lies.
    Comes our Lord, Immanuel.   (1988)

THE FACE OF LOVE

Shepherds once knelt
to look on the face of love,
and the seekers of light
found God's smile in a star.
Now the season of joy comes again.   (1987)

SEASON OF FAITH

Christmas should be
a season of faith, not fantasy,
far more than a delicate dream
devoid of reality.

For Christmas is rooted in love
and anchored in certainty.
The Child who was born is still our hope,
now as then—and for all eternity.   (1982)

WHEN WINTER COMES

Watch, when winter comes,
for the miracle of Christmas
stretching from stable to star.
    Watch, and let the miracle find you,
    wherever you are.   (1978)

THE SILVER SEASON

This is the silver season
when snow sculptures iced by the moon
mirror the marvel of stars.
    O lovely time for a Savior's birth
    and promise of peace on earth.   (1982)

A ROSE IN WINTER

In the harsh soil a flower grows.
In the dark winter blooms a rose.
So Jesus came, a gift from heaven.
So love is born, and grace is given.   (1985)

 ## BETHLEHEM

In Jesus' eyes his mother could see
All the stars in God's galaxy.

In Jesus' cry his mother could hear
Music that came from another sphere.

In Jesus' hands his mother could feel
A caring touch and power to heal.

In Jesus' heart his mother could find
A source of love for all humankind.

So she wrapped him warm and sang him to sleep,
A gift from God to treasure and keep.   (1986)

ONCE ON A CHILL DECEMBER MORN

Once on a chill December morn
the world came to a silent halt
and the land seemed frozen in a frame
where it was neither night or day.
It may have been no more than a second
when the pulse of the past was suspended
and the future waited to be born.
While the earth was quiet,
as if in a solemn secret,
the old age died, and a new era began.

LOOK FOR THE CHILD

You look for peace on earth?
Then stop by that stable where parents watch;
And scan the circle of love they form
With shepherds and sages, oxen and cattle;
And look for the child in the center,
With God in his heart.   (1982)

CRADLE THE CHRIST-CHILD

Cradle the Christ-child in your heart
    This day of days,
So that love will move in and never depart,
And peace find a home, and visions start—
    And songs of praise.   (1982)

WHEN LOVE WAS BORN

The stars
the scattered stars
must all have danced
together into one great light
that night
when love was born.   (1970)

THE GIFT OF GRACE

No shepherd's staff,
　　no angel's song,
　　　　no wise man's gift
　　　　　　to bring along—
　　　　　　　　how can I dare
　　　　　　　　　　approach his bed
　　　　　　　　　　　　to see the light
　　　　　　　　　　　　　　around his head?

Not what I bring
　　but what I need—
　　　　this is the plea
　　　　　　the Child will heed.
　　　　　　　　So let me kneel
　　　　　　　　　　before his face
　　　　　　　　　　　　to ask from God
　　　　　　　　　　　　　　the gift of grace.　　　　(1982)

HOLY NIGHT

Across the silent fields where sheep have grazed
The guardians of the flocks glance near and far;
During their faithful vigil, eyes upraised,
They see the black night brightened by a star.

Then light explodes—as if a million spheres
Should burst in galaxies from east to west
And unexpected brilliance summons fears
Enough to fill an awe-struck shepherd's breast.

So on this night above the Bethlehem plain
The glory of the Lord shines all around
And echoes of angelic song remain
Long after Judah's hills give up their sound.

O watchers of the heavens filled with light,
Remember long the splendor of this night.

(1958)

COME TO THE STABLE

Where would you look for a king—in a stable?
Where would you find a prince—in a stall?

In Bethlehem the town was packed;
the inn was crowded, the streets were jammed;
the homes were filled with invited guests—
and who could blame a harried innkeeper
for turning away a young couple
who had no reservation?

Where would you look for the Savior of the world?
Surely not in a stable, surely not in a stall?

In our town the stores were cluttered;
the holiday crowds moved restlessly back and forth;
the homes were busy with seasonal preparations—
and who could blame a weary parent
for failing to remember
whose birthday they were celebrating?

Where would you look for a king—in a stable?
Where would you find a prince—in a stall?

In Bethlehem the revelers danced all night long
and the guests in the inn slept late the next morning,
unaware of events that changed the world's history—
yet shepherds on a nearby hill heard the tidings;
Keeping watch, they heard the great invitation:
"Come to the stable; come, meet the newborn King."

In our town the celebrations still continue,
and the holiday guests wake wearily in the morning,
unaware, even yet, of events that change history.
But a few are alert, keeping watch and waiting.
They still hear a song; they still see a star;

they still respond to the great invitation:
"Come to the stable; come, meet the newborn King."

Where would you look for the Savior of the world?
Come to the stable; come to the stall.
Make a manger bed for the king deep down in your heart,
and here he will reign for ever and ever. (1960)

CHRISTMAS MORN

Oh, what do you treasure in your heart.
Mary of Nazareth, what do you ponder?
Is the travail over, the pain forgotten,
That you gaze on the child with eyes of wonder?

Did you hear last night the angel song
That flooded the earth with peace and joy?
Or were your ears bent low to heed
The cries that came from a new-born boy?

Did you listen in awe to the shepherds' story?
And did you marvel to see the star?
Or were you watching lest He be wearied
By too many visitors come from afar?

Now that the night, most strange, most holy,
Yields to the day and the child lies sleeping,
What do you keep in the depths of your heart
As you ponder and pray, your vigil keeping?
(1952)

A STAR OF HOPE

Foxes had holes
and birds their nests,
but the son of God
found no room in the city
nor a home under a tyrant.
He had only a covering of stars
and the love of God.

What do the homeless see
who wait today as refugees,
barefooted, hungry, shivering?
A star of hope
and rest on their flight?
Or never a light to pierce their night?

A CHRISTMAS CONFESSION

We were heavy with sorrow, but joy interrupted.
We were deep in the night, but a star appeared.
We were silent with sadness, but the heavens rang.

We were hardened by conflict, but love intervened,
We were frightened by shadows, but light took them
    away.
We were haunted by fears, but a child brought us hope.

We were dismal and defeated, but faith set us on fire.
We were weary and complaining, but our hearts
    discovered praise.
We were doubtful and confused, but a door to life was
    opened.

We were arrogant and angry, but his innocence disarmed
    us.
We were cruel, crude and clumsy, but his grace made all
    things new.
We were selfish, narrow, greedy, but we had to share his
    joy.

We were sheep who lost our way, but the shepherd knew
    our names.
We were folk without a country, but our kingdom came
    to us.
We were children far from home, but God sent his Son to
    guide.   (1970)

CHRISTMAS EVE, 1940

Will the angels sing on the hills tonight
    When the world is weary with war?
Will they sing again of peace on earth?
    Will the shepherds hear them once more?

Will the wise men see the star tonight
    While the fires of hate burn high?
Will they bring to the child their gifts of love?
    Will they find his star in the sky?

Will the Lord God intervene tonight
    To halt the hatred of men?
Or will this night of horror spread
    To cripple the world again?

To the ears of faith the angels sing;
    To the eyes of hope the star leads on;
To the hearts who wait the Lord God speaks;
    To the world he gives his son.   (1940)

V. Hymns and Other Songs to Sing

MOVE IN OUR MIDST

Move in our midst, thou Spirit of God.
Go with us down from thy holy hill.
Walk with us through the storm and the calm.
Spirit of God, go thou with us still.

Touch thou our hands to lead us aright.
Guide us forever, show us thy way.
Transform our darkness into thy light.
Spirit of God, lead thou us today.

Strike from our feet the fetters that bind.
Lift from our lives the weight of our wrong.
Teach us to love with heart, soul and mind.
Spirit of God, thy love makes us strong.

Kindle our hearts to burn with thy flame.
Raise up thy banners high in this hour.
Stir us to build new worlds in thy name.
Spirit of God, O send us thy power!

(1942,1949)

O GIVER OF DELIGHTFUL FIELDS

O Giver of delightful fields
    That stretch in green fertility,
O Sender of the rain and wind,
    Who made the mountain, sky and sea,
It is your soil we live upon,
    O Lord of harvests soon to fall;
Give unto us who walk this land
    The will to make you Lord of all.

Grant strength to serve humanity,
    To feed the hungering multitude,
To share your mercy, seeking those
    Whose lips, whose souls cry out for food.
O make us like Him who had naught
    But love for enemy and friend,
Who turned defeat to victory
    And lived to triumph in the end.

Grant us the will to share in full
    Our rich abundance without greed.
Grant us the spirit to deny
    Ourselves to meet another's need.
O give us eyes to look beyond
    Our little corner of the earth,
To see in faith a world reborn,
    Renewed in beauty and in worth.   (1943)

O MASTER, MAY MY DAYS BE SPENT

O Master, may my days be spent only for thee,
As thou didst give thy years of youth, living for me.
So let me serve thee, loving neighbor and God,
In deep devotion walking where thou hast trod.

O Jesus, may my hands be skilled, working for thee,
As thine were trained to touch the blind, making them
 see.
So let my fingers carry healing and balm
That they who suffer may be filled with thy calm.

O Savior, may my voice be raised, speaking for thee,
As thou didst win the hearts of men, setting them free.
So let me witness what thy power can prove;
So let me call men to thy kingdom of love.

O Lord of life and beauty, thou livest for me;
As thou didst serve thy Father, thy servant I'd be.
So in this darkness, let me herald thy light,
That with its coming, dawn will banish the night.

(1948)

GOD OF THE MOVING YEARS

God of the moving years,
God of the marching days,
Thy music on our ears
Shall turn our fears to praise.
God of each singing heart,
God of each silent voice,
Thy beauty stands apart,
Above, beyond all art.
Accept the song we raise;
Let men rejoice.

God of eternal peace,
God of undying life,
Thy mercy will not cease
To bring release from strife.
God of each hungering soul,
God of each searching mind,
Thy laws alone control
The power to make us whole.
Thou art the light of life
For all mankind.   (1948)

O CHRIST, WE CLIMB THE HILL WITH THEE

O Christ, we climb the hill with thee,
Thou Master of the upward way.
We scale the heights that we may see
Thy vision of the coming day.

Show us thy kingdom, thou our king.
Point out the paths of peace and right.
Though feet are weary, hearts will sing;
We climb into thy glorious light.

Give us the courage of thy cross,
To dare to live and die for thee,
To walk through fire, to suffer loss,
In faith that keeps us strong and free.

New worlds of beauty greet our eyes
As far horizons now we see.
O Master of the hills that rise
To unknown heights, we climb with thee.

(1949)

LORD OF LOVELINESS

Lord of loveliness, all beauty
    Bears your touch and shows your trace,
And all goodness gains its glory
    Through your purity and grace.
O that darkened eyes would open
    To the smiling of your face;
O that we might see your image
    In the hearts of every race.

Lord of lowliness, so humble,
    Who, to wash our feet knelt down,
Lord of love, who died forgiving,
    Making of your cross a crown,
O redeem us of our folly,
    Save us from our pride of sin;
O remove our selfish seeking,
    Cleanse our hearts and enter in.

Lord of life, O let your power
    Still direct us in your ways.
Let your light so clear and golden
    Now illumine all our days.
Not for safety or protection
    Shall we seek your light and power,
But to gird our lives for action
    In your kingdom, in this hour.   (1949)

BREAD OF LIFE

Bread of life, whose body, broken,
Feeds the hunger of my heart,
May the thanks that you have spoken
Bless each loaf I break apart.

Let these hands now calmly folding
Speak my gratitude for grace
Lest the treasure I am holding
Disappear before my face.

Lord, I welcome you to table;
Grace my supper ever new.
With your feast of love enable
Every guest to live for you.   (1952)

ETERNAL ARE THE WORDS

O thou who biddest every heart rejoice,
Eternal are the words that speak of thee.
From age to age thou hast not lacked a voice
To teach the truth that sets all people free.

Thy word, O God, is still our heritage,
Bearing thee witness when our voices fail.
We read thy character on every page;
We trust thy promises when fears assail.

Still do thine ancient precepts guard and guide;
Still thy commandments teach us of thy love.
Thy testimonies and thy deeds abide
To stir our wills, and our slow feet to move.

O truth incarnate in the Master's face,
O love made visible on Calvary,
May we translate the glories of thy grace
In all we say, in all we do for thee.   (1952)

O LIVING LORD

O living Lord, thine was the victory
To rise in triumph over sin and death;
No stone could hold nor tomb imprison thee;
No grave could still thy spirit's vital breath.

In faith, O Lord, we share thy victory,
No longer stumbling on our shadowed ways;
We see the light of God's eternity
Piercing the storm clouds of our darkest days.

O living Lord, the truth of Easter morn
Renews our hope and sweeps our doubt aside;
Enable us to live as ones reborn,
Who walk with courage once their fears have died.

Thy church, O Lord, with grace and power endue;
Roll from its doors the stones that close it in.
Teach us to witness to thy love anew
Where people still are slaves to self and sin.

O living Lord, each hymn of praise we sing
Must speak the joy we find in serving thee.
Our hearts we yield, our gifts to thee we bring;
Thine is the kingdom, thine the victory.

(1953)

HOLY IS THE LORD

Holy, holy, holy is the Lord of hosts;
Great and marvelous are all his mighty deeds.
Earth and heaven, sea and sky his glories show;
One eternal word the vast creation heeds:
    Holy, holy, holy is the Lord our God.

Holy, holy, holy is the God most high.
Earth's foundations tremble when they hear his voice;
Yet the starry universe his power declares.
Cherubim and seraphim sing and rejoice:
    Holy, holy, holy is the Lord our God.

Holy, holy, holy is the King of kings.
High above his temple God will ever dwell.
Angels hover round about his lofty throne;
Mortals join the chorus that their praises swell:
    Holy, holy, holy is the Lord our God.

(1959)

ETERNAL SPIRIT, COME ONCE MORE

O thou eternal Spirit, come once more
To shake all sheltered hearts that hide from thee.
Come like the storm that batters every shore.
Come like the flame that burns and then sets free.

O thou disturbing Spirit, light our way
With wonders new to heaven, strange to earth.
Let vaster visions drive our dreams of day.
Until in thee we find our souls' rebirth.

O thou supporting Spirit, come and dwell;
Renew thy church and recreate that hour
Of Pentecost when on thy people fell
The rushing wind, the fire, the mighty power.

(1963)

A HYMN FOR WORLD COMMUNION

O gracious Host, whose guests have come
From south and north, from west and east,
Your welcome draws us to one home,
By invitation to one feast.

Apart we live, yet hearts are knit
In fellowship as hand meets hand.
Around one table we may sit,
One church, one company, one band.

Let none be lonely, bound, or broken;
Let none be alien to another.
We know the living Word has spoken
To claim each sister and each brother.

Though many separate ways we take,
Scattered to east, west, south, and north,
One cup we drink, one bread we break,
One table circles all the earth.   (1963)

WHY IS THE NIGHT SO STILL?

Why is the night so still, so holy?
Why have the shepherds come to town?
They come to see a child born lowly,
Here in a manger, bedded down.

Why do the patient beasts stand quiet?
Why do they honor a child so small?
They are at peace with all creation,
Knowing God loves them, who loves us all.

Why is one star so bright, so radiant?
Why are the skies ablaze with light?
It is because the child of Mary
Rests in the arms of God tonight.

Why do the heavens fill with music?
What do these angel voices tell?
They sing of Christ, the world's redeemer,
God in our midst, Immanuel.   (1966)

GIFTS FOR A KING

From out of the east the astrologers came,
  Out of the east.
They sought for a ruler without any name,
  Out of the east.
They looked for a king who was also a child,
For one who would reign and yet be mild,
The greatest and least, whether king or child,
  Greatest and least.

What brings you from far, you who search out the skies?
  What brings you far?
And what is the sign of the ruler so wise,
  Who brings you far?
"A flame in the sky and a fire in the night,
A comet's tail and a meteor's flight,
A rising star, his own star so bright,
  His rising star."

And where do you ride to find such majesty?
  Where do you ride?
For surely his home is as royal as he,
  Where do you ride?
"We stay no longer in Jerusalem,
But journey onward to Bethlehem.
His star will guide us to find his home;
  His star will guide."

What gifts do you bring for the child that you seek?
  What do you bring?
What gifts will do honor for one who is meek?
  What do you bring?
"Gold, frankincense and myrrh have we,
And with them our love and loyalty,
Our gifts for a king who will set us free,
  Gifts for a king."   (1968)

87

TWELVE DAYS OF CHRISTMAS

On the first day of Christmas
God gives us all a child,
A baby, a brother,
A friend both meek and mild.

On the second day of Christmas
God sorrows at our strife.
The marvel, the wonder,
God turns our death to life.

On the third day of Christmas
God lifts a flaming star
For all who are seeking.
God finds them where they are.

On the fourth day of Christmas
The heavens burn with light.
No shadow, no darkness
Can turn that day to night.

On the fifth day of Christmas
The skies break into song.
Such singing, such music
Allows no place for wrong.

On the sixth day of Christmas
God wraps the earth in joy.
Come shepherds, come sages
To honor Mary's boy.

On the seventh day of Christmas
God gives the world its king.
Let all of God's people
Begin and ever sing.

On the eighth day of Christmas
God says, "Let hatred cease.
This child and his kingdom
Shall bring the world its peace."

On the ninth day of Christmas
God speaks a mighty word.
The burdened, the lonely
Find welcome with their Lord.

On the tenth day of Christmas
God says, "Good folk, look up!
Let fears be forgotten
And trust this child of hope."

On the eleventh day of Christmas
God's purpose is unfurled.
A Savior is given,
For God so loves the world.

On the twelfth day of Christmas
What shall this Savior prove?
His mission is mercy,
His ministry is love.   (1969)

GOOD NEWS FOR YOU

Refrain:
> There's good news for you, good news,
> Good news for you and all the world.
> There's a time of joy, great joy,
> Great joy for you and all the world.

1. Don't be scared, you shepherds;
    God has heard you praying.
    Listen to the angels;
    Hear what they are saying.

2. Hear the song of glory,
    Sung from highest heaven
    For the baby Jesus,
    Who to earth is given.

3. You can cease your crying;
    Warfare will be ending.
    Peace on earth is promised;
    God a Son is sending.

4. He's a child for holding.
    He's a star for guiding.
    He's the hope you long for.
    He is love abiding.   (1970)

TOO LONG THE YEAR

Too long the year has hid from sight
Its promise of that morning light
Which can dissolve the darkest night.
    O come, O come, Immanuel.

At last the time of hope draws near,
The dawning of a day so clear
That timid hearts will lose their fear
    And welcome you, Immanuel.

Lord, grant that our awaking eyes
Reflect the radiance of your skies
And turn from sleep to glad surprise.
    O come to us, Immanuel.

Lord, hatreds burden us with pain,
But love can wash away their stain
And joyful music sound again.
    O come, O come, Immanuel.   (1970)

O GOD OF MYSTERY AND MIGHT

O God of mystery and might,
Great mover of the stars in flight,
Alert our hearts to apprehend
The silent messages you send.

Lord, set our ears to listening
For reasons in each season's spring;
And teach our minds to meditate
Longer on love, while passions wait.

O God of tenderness and trust,
Whose ways are merciful and just,
Lest we be overcome with gain
Bind us into each other's pain.

From pride and pretense set us free
To walk in truth's integrity.
O grant us grace to reach, to give,
To touch the dream by which we live.   (1970)

SING OF LOVE

Dark are the ways where blindly we have run;
Yet when we stumble, God still leads us on.
Sharp eyes we need to penetrate our gloom.
The arms of God are here to lift and warm.

> Come sing , my friends, sing of love.
> Shout your joy in a jubilant song,
> For God so loves this world of pain
> He bathes its sorrows in his rain,
> And heals all the hungers that remain,
> So deep is God's love, so strong.

When we had lost our way, and weary stood,
One Friend we found who lightened every load.
Jesus would not condemn us for our sins;
Instead he said, "Come follow! Life begins!"

> Then sing, my friends, sing of love.
> Shout your joy in a jubilant song,
> For God would break each fearful chain
> And grant to each a life to gain,
> Turn night into morning light again,
> So deep is God's love, so strong.

O Lord, your gifts are prompted by your grace;
Your kingdom claims all nations and each race.
Lift up our hearts, and teach our tongues to share
This love of yours with people everywhere.

> Then sing, my friends, sing of love.
> Shout your joy in a jubilant song,
> For God has said, "You are set free."
> Sisters and brothers we can be
> For time and for all eternity,
> So deep is God's love, so strong. (1971)

IF STARS WERE TO SING

(A Mother's Lullaby)

If stars were like angels,
This night would sing,
   If stars were like angels.
If stars were to sing,
The heavens would ring,
   If stars were like angels.

O child of my pain, O love of my heart,
   O life of my own life-giving,
You are the music and you are the joy
   To make each day worth living.

O babe in a manger, child of my dreams,
   So fragile, so tender, now sleeping,
You are the promise and you are the sign
   That God a good watch is keeping.

If stars were like angels,
If stars were to sing,
They would glorify God
And welcome their king
   If stars were to sing.   (1973)

GO WALK IN THE WORLD

Go walk in the world with the Spirit's fire;
Its glowing will light you and lead you far.
Let Christ be your fervor, your burning desire,
Your sunlight by day, in darkness your star.

Start out where you live, in spite of your fears,
And go where God points though the way seems long.
Go forth amid anguish and stand amid tears;
The Lord is your compass, your comfort, your song.

Go walk in the world where the millions wait,
So hungry for healing, so needful of grace.
They know not God's mercy; they fear for their fate.
Go show them the beauty that shines in God's face.

Let peace be your practice and faith be your flame.
No tomb can dissuade you, nor death yet destroy
Your sense of God's presence, your trust in God's name.
Go walk in the world with a heart full of joy.

(1973)

MINE ARE THE HUNGRY

Brothers and sisters of mine are the hungry
Who sigh in their sorrow and weep in their pain.
Sisters and brothers of mine are the homeless
Who wait without shelter from wind and from rain.

Strangers and neighbors, they claim my attention;
They sleep by my doorstep, they sit by my bed.
Neighbors and strangers, their anguish concerns me,
And I must not feast till the hungry are fed.

People are they, men and women and children,
And each has a heart keeping time with my own.
People are they, persons made in God's image;
So what shall I offer them, bread or a stone?

Lord of all living, we make our confession:
Too long we have wasted the wealth of our lands.
Lord of all loving, renew our compassion
And open our hearts while we reach out our hands.

(1974)

STRANGERS NO MORE

Come, walk with me, we'll praise the Lord together,
    As we join song to song and prayer to prayer.
    Come, take my hand, and we will work together
    By lifting all the burdens we can share.

Refrain:
    For we are strangers no more, but members of one
        family;
    Strangers no more, but part of one humanity;
    Strangers no more, we're neighbors to each other now;
    Strangers no more, we're sisters and we're brothers
        now.

Where differing cultures meet we'll serve together.
    Where hatred rages we will strive for peace.
    Come, take my hand, and we will pray together
    That justice come and strife and warfare cease.

Refrain:

There is a love that binds the world together,
    A love that seeks the last, the lost, the least.
    One day that love will bring us all together
    In Christ from south and north, from west and east.

Refrain: (1979)

WHAT CHILD IS THIS?

What child is this whose life is torn
By pain and devastation,
Who turns to you a face forlorn,
In need of consolation?

> (Refrain)
>> This, this is a child of God,
>> Who waits for you to help and heal.
>> Haste, haste to bring your gifts
>> In the name of the Son of Mary.

What child is this who lives distressed
By illness and starvation,
Who looks in vain for health and rest
And promise of salvation?

Come, people who still sing and pray
To Jesus in a manger,
Remember how he taught each day
No child should be a stranger.   (1981)

O VOICE OF GOD, SPEAK TO YOUR PEOPLE

O voice of God, speak to your people now
That they go forward to their promised land
Where fields lie fertile, eager for the plow,
And harvests beckon to each willing hand.

The light of Christ shines through our wilderness
To point us, step by step, along our way.
Though we may stumble, still our paths we press,
Firm in the faith that opens each new day.

We claim the witness of our pioneers,
Prophets and martyrs, saints in common clay,
Whose dreams were stronger than their host of
    fears,
Who, daring unknown dangers, marked our way.

O God of journeys, send us forth in joy
With hands of healing for the world's distress.
Direct our feet, our hearts and minds employ.
We seek your kingdom and its righteousness.

(1986)

PRAISE, I WILL PRAISE YOU, LORD

Praise, I will praise you, Lord, with all my heart.
O God, I will tell the wonders of your ways,
And glorify your name.

Praise, I will praise you, Lord, with all my heart.
In you I will find the source of all my joy,
Alleluia! (1988)

Note: The text is a translation of *Je Louerai l'Eternel*, by Claude Fraysse.

O God Who comes,
Be With All Those Who Wait

O God who comes, be with all those who wait
With eager longing for your day of light.
Your time draws near; the hour is not too late
For faith to banish fear and end our night.

Come as the Child whose birth the heavens greet.
Come as the Prophet who confronts our strife.
Come as the Servant who would wash our feet.
Come as the Savior who turns death to life.

Grant us the grace to look discerningly
For signs of Christ's revealing. He is nigh!
Waiting, we sense the coming majesty,
And hints of alleluias fill our sky. (1990)

NOTES ON HYMNS AND SONGS

Move in Our Midst   Meter: 11.11.11.11.

The first two stanzas were written in 1942 and set to the tune "Pine Glen" by Perry L. Huffaker. The other stanzas were written in 1949. Chosen for the 1951 *Brethren Hymnal* (No. 225), the hymn was introduced at the 1950 Church of the Brethren Annual Conference and later included in several hymnals and collections in: *Because We Are One People* (No. 58), published in 1974 by Ecumenical Women's Centers; in *Sing Shalom*, published in 1975 by the United Church of Christ; in *Songs of Light* (No. 23), published in 1977 by Plough Publishing House; and in *Hymnal Sampler* (No. 96), published in 1989 by The Hymnal Project. The text has been featured in song sheets, songsters, cards, posters, and newspapers. It has been translated into Spanish, reprinted in India, and used by churches in New Zealand.

O Giver of Delightful Fields   Meter: 8.8.8.8.D.

Written as a "Prayer for America," this text appeared first as a poem in *Our Young People*, July 3, 1943. It was included as No. 596 in the *Brethren Hymnal*, 1951.

O Master,   Meter: 11.11.11.11.
May My Days Be Spent

The text was written in 1948 to match a tune written earlier, a tune harmonized later by Perry L. Huffaker. The hymn appeared as No. 370 in the 1951 *Brethren Hymnal* and as No. 446 in *The Hymnal of the Evangelical United Brethren Church* (1957).

God of the Moving Years   Meter: 12.12.12.12.11.

Set to the tune "Spring Run," by Perry L. Huffaker, the text was included in the 1951 *Brethren Hymnal* (No. 72) and, with a different tune, in *Hymnbook for Christian Worship* (No. 37), a hymnal for Disciples of Christ and American Baptist churches (1970).

O Christ, We Climb the Hill With Thee

Meter: 8.8.8.8.

The text was written around 1948 to match the tune "Theodore" by Peter Lutkin and included as No. 408 in the 1951 *Brethren Hymnal*. With a different tune the text appears as No. 207 in *Hymnbook for Christian Worship* (1970).

Lord of Loveliness

Meter: 8.7.8.7.D

Set to the tune "Highland Avenue," by Nevin W. Fisher, this text was in the *Brethren Hymnal*, 1951.

Bread of Life

Meter: 8.7.8.7.

Written originally as a "Grace Before Meals" for the cover of the November 19, 1955 *Gospel Messenger*, this text was set to the tune "Rohrer" by Wilbur Brumbaugh. The hymn was printed in the *Gospel Messenger* for November 28, 1962 and the text reprinted in the *Sabbath Recorder* (Seventh Day Baptists) May 21, 1962. The entire hymn was included in the *Brethren Songbook*, 1962.

Eternal Are the Words

Meter: 10.10.10.10.

The text was written for the editorial page of the *Gospel Messenger* for September 27, 1952 on the occasion of the publication of the Revised Standard Version of the Bible.

O Living Lord

Meter: 10.10.10.10.

Originally written as "A Hymn to the Living Lord" for the editorial page of the April 4, 1953 *Gospel Messenger*, the text was set to music by two Brethren composers but never included in any published collection.

Holy Is the Lord

Meter 11.11.11.11.11.

These words were first printed as a poem on the editorial page of the March 14, 1959 *Gospel Messenger* with the title, "Song of the Seraphim."

Eternal Spirit, Come Once More

Meter: 10.10.10.10.

Entitled "Invocation for Pentecost," these lines were printed in the June 1, 1963 *Gospel Messenger* and in the May 22, 1969 issue of *Messenger*. Copyright held by Brethren Press, 1969.

A Hymn for World Communion

Meter: 8.8.8.8.

Originally written as a meditation for World Communion Sunday (*Gospel Messenger*, October 5, 1963) these lines were later altered to make them more inclusive and less archaic.

Why Is the Night So Still?

Meter: 9.8.9.8.

Together with a tune by Wilbur Brumbaugh, the text appeared in the *Gospel Messenger* and the Church of the Brethren *Leader* in the early 1960s, it was then issued as a song sheet and appeared with an additional stanza in *Messenger*, December, 1977. It was later included in the *Brethren Songbook*. Copyright held by the Church of the Brethren General Board, 1966.

Gifts for a King

Meter: Irregular

This text, matched to a tune by Wilbur Brumbaugh, appeared in the December 5, 1968 issue of *Messenger* and was included in the *Brethren Songbook*. Copyright held by the Church of the Brethren General Board, 1968.

Twelve Days of Christmas

Meter: 7.6.6.6.

The text and tune by Kenneth Morse, with harmonization by Wilbur Brumbaugh, were introduced as a new Christmas carol in a special supplement to a December, 1969 issue of *Messenger* and distributed also as a song sheet. Copyright held by the Church of the Brethren General Board, 1969.

Good News for You

Meter: 6.6.6.6. with refrain

Set to a tune by Wilbur Brumbaugh, the text appeared in *Messenger*, December 17, 1970, and soon after in the *Brethren Songbook*. Copyright held by the Church of the Brethren General Board, 1970.

Too Long the Year   Meter: 8.8.8.8.

These lines were written as an advent hymn for use on a November 1970 Church of the Brethren Sunday bulletin.

O God of Mystery and Might   Meter: 8.8.8.8.

This text, set to a tune by Wilbur Brumbaugh, appeared in *Messenger* February 1, 1971. In 1974 it was published in the *Brethren Songbook*. Copyright held by the Church of the Brethren General Board, 1970.

Sing of Love   Meter: 10,10,10,10, with Refrain.

This text, with music by Wilbur Brumbaugh, was printed in the August 1, 1971 issue of *Messenger*. The song was included in the first edition of the *Brethren Songbook*. Copyright held by by the Church of the Brethren General Board, 1971.

If Stars Were to Sing   Meter: Irregular.

Intended as a Christmas lullaby, these words were set to music by Dianne Morningstar. The song was included in later editions of the *Brethren Songbook*. Copyright held by Brethren Press, 1979.

Go Walk in the World   Meter: Irregular.

These lines were printed on a Church of the Brethren Sunday bulletin in December, 1974.

Mine Are the Hungry   Meter: 11.11.11.11.

Written in 1974, this text was set to music by Wilbur Brumbaugh and featured in Brethren publications, including a Sunday bulletin in November 1975. It was used widely by the Christian Rural Overseas Program and various ecumenical groups as a songsheet and program resource related to world hunger. It was chosen as the theme song for American Baptist Women in 1977-1979. It was published in the *Journal of Stewardship* of the National Council of Churches in 1978. The text appears in several hymnals and song collections: the *Brethren Songbook*; *Sing Shalom*, published by the United Church of Christ, 1977; *Sisters and Brothers Sing*, published in 1977; *Hymns of the Saints*, published by the Reorganized Church of the Latter Day Saints, 1981; *Psalter Hymnal*, published by the Christian Reformed Church, 1987; *Hymnal Sampler*, published by Hymnal Project, 1989; and *Banquet of Praise*, published by Bread for the World, 1990. Copyright held by Brethren Press, 1974.

Strangers No More
Meter: 11.10.11.10.
with Refrain.

The text was written, with a tune by Dianne Morningstar, to introduce a slide interpretation of world ministries at the 1979 Church of the Brethren Annual Conference. It was published first as a song sheet in 1979 by Daystar Associates, then in the *Brethren Songbook*. It was included in *Singing for Peace*, published by Hope Publishing Company in 1986; and in *Hymnal Sampler*. Copyright by Kenneth I. Morse, 1979.

What Child Is This?
Meter: 8.7.8.7.
with Refrain.

The words may be sung to the tune "Greensleeves." They appeared in *Agenda* near the end of 1981.

Praise, I Will Praise You, Lord
Meter: Irregular.

The English text is a translation of a French song, "Je Louerai l'Eternel," by Claude Fraysse. It appears in the *Hymnal Sampler*. Copyright held by the Hymnal Project, 1989.

O God Who Comes, Be With All Those Who Wait
Meter: 10.10.10.10.

This text was printed in the Church of the Brethren Living Word bulletin for December 2, 1990 for use as an Advent hymn.

Index of Titles and First Lines

(First lines in italics)

I

J

L

M